# EASY
# ITALIAN
# DISHES

# EASY ITALIAN DISHES

SAFEWAY/GOOD HOUSEKEEPING

## COOKERY NOTES

*All spoon measures are level unless otherwise stated.*

*Size 2 eggs should be used except when otherwise stated.*

*Granulated sugar is used unless otherwise stated.*

*The oven should be preheated to the required temperature unless otherwise stated.*

Published exclusively for
Safeway
6 Millington Road, Hayes, Middlesex UB3 4AY
by Ebury Press
A division of Random House
20 Vauxhall Bridge Road
London SW1V 2SA

First published 1994

Edited by Julia Canning and Louise Steele
Recipes by Good Housekeeping Institute and Linda Frazer
Designed by Behram Kapadia
Photography by Michelle Garrett
Food stylist Liz Trigg

The paper in this book is acid-free

Typeset by Textype Typesetters, Cambridge
Printed in Italy

ISBN 0-09-182498-2

# CONTENTS

# FOREWORD

Welcome to *Easy Italian Dishes*, part of the exciting new *Cooking Around the World* series produced in association with Safeway.

Each of the six books in this unique series is dedicated to one of the countries of the world most renowned for its mouthwatering cuisine. All the recipes have been double tested by the cooks in the Good Housekeeping Institute using Safeway's quality produce.

Presented in a clear, step-by-step format, many of the recipes are quick and easy enough to suit the pace of hectic modern living, although anyone looking to create an exotic feast for a really special occasion will not be disappointed.

To take the 'worry factor' out of using new ingredients, you will find tips on how to identify, select and prepare exotic fruit and vegetables, aromatic herbs and spices and other produce in the introductory pages.

Through the *Cooking Around the World* series you can bring the tastes and flavours of six fascinating countries to your table.

MOYRA FRASER
Cookery Editor
*Good Housekeeping*

# INTRODUCTION

Capturing the delicious and distinctive flavours of Italian cookery is easy when you have the right ingredients at your fingertips. Fortunately, today there is an excellent choice of Italian products available, ranging from intriguing pasta shapes and unusual-tasting hams to mouthwatering cheeses and glorious vegetables, bursting with freshness. Pick and choose from the following list to create delicious meals that are full of the sunny taste of Italy.

## PASTA

This popular Italian ingredient, which is made from hard durum wheat, is now available in a wide range of shapes and sizes, in both fresh and dried forms. Coloured pasta is also available and is good for adding interest to meals – green pasta (*pasta verde*) is flavoured with spinach, while pink or red pasta (*pasta rosso*) is flavoured with tomatoes. Wholewheat pasta contains more fibre than the white version and is enjoyed for its delicious flavour and chewy texture.

**LONG PASTA** Perfect for serving with lighter sauces, long pasta comes in a variety of widths, including spaghetti (thin strings); vermicelli (thin spaghetti); capellini (extra fine strings); and tagliatelle (flat ribbons). Fettucine is the Roman version of tagliatelle. Lasagne is a broad flat noodle and is always baked in the oven (*al forno*), layered with sauce.

**SHORT PASTA** The cut pasta and pasta shapes included in this group are ideal for serving with heavier sauces which contain large chunks of meat and fish. They are also excellent for baked dishes. Choose from cannelloni (hollow tubes for stuffing); conchiglie (seashells); farfalle (bows); fusilli (spirals); penne (hollow pasta shaped like quills); or maccheroni (elbow maceroni, short curved tubes). Filled pasta shapes such as tortellini (twisted rings or navels) and ravioli (small rounds or squares) are good served with thin sauce or just melted butter and a sprinkling of herbs and grated Parmesan.

## HOMEMADE PASTA

Nothing quite compares with the excellent flavour, texture and freshness of homemade pasta. If you intend making pasta regularly, it makes sense to buy a pasta machine which makes easy work of the rolling process. Electric machines are available but they are expensive – a far better buy is the hand operated type which does the job splendidly and is simplicity itself to use.

To roll pasta dough by hand, use a good rolling pin – the best kinds are those with tapered ends and made of beechwood. Roll the dough on a floured surface to a large rectangle until it is almost paper thin (this is hard work and takes time, so do be patient – and remember that practice makes perfect). Transfer the sheet of dough to a tea-towel sprinkled with flour and leave to rest for about 1 hour, according to the temperature and humidity of the room. Do not allow the pasta to dry out too much or it becomes tough and difficult to cut neatly. Use a sharp knife or a pastry or pasta wheel for cutting. Spread out the pasta on a floured tea-towel and use within 24 hours.

## ARBORIO RICE

To achieve the correct consistency for authentic Italian risotto it is essential to use arborio rice – a special short-grain rice which, when cooked in the proper way, gives a deliciously creamy, almost sticky result – just perfect for risotto.

## ITALIAN CHEESES

**PARMESAN** is probably the most famous of all Italian cheeses. Whenever possible, buy this cheese by the piece for grating, as the ready-grated type is drier and tends to have less flavour. Genuine Parmesan must bear the stamp Parmigiano Reggiano on its rind, so check this before buying. Look for cheese which is pale buff-yellow in colour, and not too crumbly in texture.

**GORGONZOLA** is a creamy, blue-veined cheese with a mild, tangy flavour. It is excellent as a table cheese and in cooked and uncooked dishes.

**MASCARPONE** is a thick and creamy dessert cheese. It is delicious served with fruits or used as an ingredient in desserts.

**MOZZARELLA** is a soft, round cheese sold in its own whey. It was originally made from buffalo's milk, but now more commonly from cow's milk or a mixture of both. Make sure you use Italian mozzarella to enjoy its fine flavour. It is eaten in salads and antipasto, or cooked in pizza toppings, baked dishes and sauces.

**RICOTTA** is a fresh, moist cheese with a slightly sweetish flavour. It is mostly used in cooking and may be substituted with curd or cottage cheese when unavailable.

## SALAMI

Salami features prominently in Italian cuisine – and comes in literally hundreds of different shapes, sizes and flavours. Pepperoni, a spicy pork and beef sausage, forms a popular pizza topping.

## PARMA HAM

Prosciutto is the Italian word for ham, and Prosciutto di Parma is the most famous of all. Genuine Parma hams have been dried for at least 8 months (in some cases for as long as 2 years) which gives them a sweet, smoky flavour. Delicious used in antipasto or cooked in dishes.

## HERBS

Herbs play an essential role in Italian dishes giving them authentic flavour.

**BASIL**, surely one of Italy's favourite herbs, is used to great effect and in quantity in the now famous pesto sauce. Tomatoes have a special affinity with basil and most tomato-based soups and sauces are flavoured with this herb.

**OREGANO** (wild marjoram) is another herb much used in Italian cookery and a popular flavouring for tomato dishes, pasta sauces and pizza toppings.

## PINE KERNELS

These tiny elongated nuts with a creamy texture and delicate flavour are extremely popular with the Italians and are one of the classic ingredients in pesto sauce. Also delicious in stuffings and sprinkled over vegetable dishes, salads and pizzas.

## OLIVES

There are many different varieties available. Olives may be picked when they are green or when fully ripe and black. They are sometimes pitted, or may be stuffed.

**OLIVE OIL** Italian olive oil is regarded as one of the best in the world. There are lots of different brands to choose from, but it is always worth buying the best quality you can afford. Extra-virgin olive oil is made from the first cold pressing of olives and is rich and flavourful.

## VEGETABLES

The Italian climate produces a wealth of wonderful vegetables, including tomatoes, peppers, aubergines, courgettes, asparagus and globe artichokes – all used extensively to create the flavourful dishes associated with the country.

**TOMATOES**, whether fresh or canned, or in purée form, dominate the cooking of Italy for they are used as an essential flavouring in hundreds of dishes. The 'plum' tomato is especially juicy and full of flavour and both the fresh and canned types are popularly used for making rich and delicious sauces and toppings.

**FLORENCE FENNEL**, another popular vegetable with Italians, is a bulbous-shaped vegetable with a distinctive aniseed flavour and crisp, crunchy texture. It is delicious raw or cooked.

# STARTERS

*Designed to give the perfect start to meals, the following recipes offer an imaginative choice of dishes to suit most occasions, or may be enjoyed on their own as a tasty lunch or supper-time snack. From the tempting simplicity of Hot Crostini, to mouthwatering golden-fried seafoods in Fritto Misto, or the fresh tangy mix of juicy pears and Gorgonzola, there is something here to suit all tastes and pockets.*

# HOT CROSTINI

SERVES 6

*115 g (4 oz) sun-dried tomatoes*

*4 × 15 ml tbs olive oil*

*6 fresh basil leaves*

*6 large slices of crusty Italian-style bread, such as Ciabatta*

*black olives*

**1** Soak the sun-dried tomatoes in warm water for about 30 minutes. Drain. Place in a food processor with the olive oil and fresh basil. Blend until smooth.

**2** Toast the bread. Spread with tomato mixture and place a few olives on top. Serve immediately.

# TUSCAN BEAN SOUP

SERVES 6

*335 g (12 oz) dried cannellini beans, soaked overnight in cold water*

*4 × 15 ml tbs olive oil*

*2 large onions, skinned and roughly chopped*

*6 celery sticks, trimmed and roughly chopped*

*2 garlic cloves, skinned and crushed*

*450 g (1 lb) tomatoes, skinned and roughly chopped*

*1.4 lt (2½ pt) vegetable stock*

*1 × 15 ml tbs chopped fresh thyme*

*salt and pepper*

*freshly grated Parmesan cheese and fresh thyme, to garnish*

**1** Drain the beans, rinse thoroughly under cold running water, then tip into a large saucepan and cover with fresh water. Bring to the boil and boil rapidly for 10 minutes. Lower the heat, cover and simmer for about 50 minutes or until the beans are tender. Drain, reserving the cooking liquor.

**2** Put half the beans in a blender or food processor. Add 300 ml (10 fl oz) of the reserved cooking liquor and purée until smooth.

**3** Heat the oil in a large saucepan. Add the onions, celery and garlic and cook over a moderate heat for 5-10 minutes or until beginning to brown. Stir in the tomatoes, stock, whole beans and bean purée with the thyme. Add salt and pepper and bring to the boil.

**4** Reduce the heat, cover and simmer for about 40 minutes or until all the ingredients are tender. Serve hot, sprinkled with Parmesan cheese and thyme.

# BAGNA CAUDA

SERVES 6

*150 ml (5 fl oz) olive oil*

*75 g (3 oz) butter*

*2 garlic cloves, skinned and finely chopped*

*2 × 50 g (2 oz) cans anchovy fillets, drained and finely chopped*

*227 g bundle asparagus, trimmed and freshly cooked*

*3 globe artichokes, trimmed and freshly cooked*

*1 small cauliflower, cut into florets*

*1 large red pepper, seeded and cut into strips*

*1 large green pepper, seeded and cut into strips*

*4 carrots, peeled and cut into finger-sized sticks*

*6 celery sticks, trimmed and cut into small sticks*

*3 courgettes, trimmed and cut into finger-sized sticks*

*1 bunch radishes, trimmed*

**1** Heat the oil and butter in a saucepan until just melted. Add the garlic and cook gently for 2 minutes. Do not allow it to colour.

**2** Add the anchovies and cook very gently, stirring all the time for 10 minutes or until the anchovies dissolve into a paste.

**3** Transfer the dip to an earthenware dish and keep warm over a fondue burner or spirit lamp at the table. Each guest dips the prepared vegetables in the hot anchovy sauce.

Bagna Cauda

# TUNA FISH WITH BEANS

SERVES 4

*175 g (6 oz) dried white haricot or cannellini beans,*
*soaked overnight in cold water*

*3 × 15 ml tbs olive oil*

*1 × 15 ml tbs wine vinegar*

*salt and pepper*

*1 small red onion, skinned and finely sliced*

*200 g can tuna fish in oil, drained and flaked into*
*large chunks*

*flat leaf parsley sprigs, to garnish*

**1** Drain the beans, rinse thoroughly under cold running water, then tip into a large saucepan and cover with fresh cold water. Bring to the boil and boil rapidly for 10 minutes. Lower the heat, cover and simmer for about 50 minutes or until beans are tender. Drain.

**2** Whisk together the oil, vinegar and salt and pepper to taste. Stir into the hot beans, then cool for 15 minutes.

**3** Mix in the onion, then the tuna fish, being careful not to break it up too much. Taste and adjust seasoning, then transfer to a serving dish. Garnish with parsley sprigs just before serving.

# ITALIAN SALAMI SALAD

SERVES 4

*450 g (1 lb) tomatoes, skinned and thinly sliced*

*150 ml (5 fl oz) olive oil*

*3-4 × 15 ml tbs red wine vinegar*

*2 × 15 ml tbs chopped fresh basil*

*salt and pepper*

*¼ × 5 ml tsp sugar*

*175 g (6 oz) sliced Italian salami*

*175 g (6 oz) Mozzarella cheese*

*227 g pack fresh cooked mussels*

*2 × 50 g (2 oz) cans anchovy fillets in oil, drained and*
*soaked in milk 20 minutes*

*basil leaves, to garnish*

**1** Arrange the tomato slices, overlapping, on circular individual plates. Whisk together the oil, 3 × 15 ml tbs vinegar, half the basil and salt and pepper to taste. Add more vinegar to taste, if liked. Sprinkle the tomatoes evenly with the sugar, then pour over half the dressing.

**2** Cut the salami into thin strips, removing the skin. Arrange the salami on top of the tomatoes. Cut the cheese into strips and arrange on top of the salami. Scatter the mussels over the cheese.

**3** Drain the anchovies and pat dry. Use the anchovies to form a decorative boder on each salad. Drizzle over the remaining dressing, then refrigerate for 2-3 hours. Sprinkle with the remaining chopped basil and basil leaves just before serving.

TOP Italian Salami Salad
BOTTOM Tuna Fish with Beans

# FRITTO MISTO DI MARE

SERVES 6

*227 g pack ready-prepared seafood cocktail*

*335 g (12 oz) firm, white fish fillets, such as cod,*
*haddock or sole, skinned, and cut into long thin strips*

*12-18 large raw prawns, peeled*

*4 × 15 ml tbs seasoned flour*

*vegetable oil, for deep frying*

*lemon wedges, to garnish*

**1** Mix together the seafood cocktail with the strips of white fish and prawns. Toss all the fish in the seasoned flour.

**2** Half-fill a deep-fat fryer with oil and heat to 190°C/375°F or until a cube of day-old bread browns in 40 seconds. Add the fish pieces a few at a time and fry until crisp and golden brown. Drain on absorbent kitchen paper and keep each batch warm while frying the remainder.

**3** Divide the fish between eight warmed plates. Garnish with lemon wedges.

COOK'S TIP

Squid is traditionally used in this dish, but you can vary the ingredients as you wish – try using whitebait instead of the seafood cocktail for instance.

# STUFFED SARDINES

SERVES 4

*8 fresh sardines, gutted*

*2 × 15 ml tbs fresh white breadcrumbs*

*4 × 15 ml tbs grated Parmesan cheese*

*4 × 15 ml tbs mixed chopped fresh herbs, such as*
*thyme, parsley, oregano or marjoram*

*2 garlic cloves, skinned and crushed*

*2 sun-dried tomatoes in oil, drained and*
*finely chopped*

*salt and pepper*

*2 × 15 ml tbs extra-virgin olive oil*

**1** Cut the heads from the sardines and then slit the fish open along the belly to the tail. Cut one or two shallow slashes in the sides of the sardines, then wipe them with absorbent kitchen paper and set aside.

**2** Mix together the breadcrumbs, Parmesan, herbs, garlic and sun-dried tomatoes and season to taste with salt and pepper. Stir in the olive oil and use to stuff the sardines, pressing them gently back into shape.

**3** Brush a little oil over a shallow ovenproof dish, lay the fish in the dish, season with salt and pepper and bake in the oven at 180°C/350°F/Gas Mark 4 for 20 minutes. Serve at once.

TOP Stuffed Sardines
BOTTOM Fritto Misto di Mare

# GORGONZOLA-STUFFED PEARS

### SERVES 4

115 g (4 oz) Gorgonzola cheese, at room temperature

25 g (1 oz) unsalted butter, softened

50 g (2 oz) shelled walnuts, finely chopped

freshly ground black pepper

150 ml (5 fl oz) thick mayonnaise

1 × 15 ml tbs tarragon vinegar

2 ripe firm pears, such as Packham

juice of ½ lemon

fresh mint sprigs, to garnish

1 Make the stuffing mixture. Work half the cheese and the butter together with a fork. Add half of the walnuts and pepper to taste and mix together until well combined. (Do not add salt as the cheese is quite salty enough.)

2 Soften the remaining cheese and work it into the mayonnaise. Stir the tarragon vinegar into the mayonnaise mixture to thin it down to a light coating consistency. If too thick, add a little more vinegar. Taste and adjust the seasoning.

3 Peel the pears and, using a sharp knife, cut each one in half lengthways. Scoop out the cores and a little of the surrounding flesh with a sharp-edged teaspoon. Immediately brush lemon juice over the exposed flesh to prevent discoloration. Fill the scooped-out centres of the pears with the Gorgonzola stuffing mixture.

4 To serve, place one pear half, cut side down, on each individual serving plate. Coat the pears with the mayonnaise, then sprinkle with the remaining chopped walnuts. Serve immediately, garnished with mint sprigs.

Gorgonzola-stuffed Pears

# AUBERGINE CANNELLONI

SERVES 4

| |
| --- |
| *2 aubergines, each weighing about 250 g (9 oz)* |
| *about 75 ml (3 fl oz) extra-virgin olive oil* |
| *225 g (8 oz) ricotta cheese* |
| *50 g (2 oz) Parmesan cheese, freshly grated* |
| *1 × 15 ml tbs finely shredded fresh basil leaves* |
| *freshly grated Parmesan cheese and fresh basil leaves, to garnish* |
| *TOMATO SAUCE* |
| *1 × 15 ml tbs extra-virgin olive oil* |
| *1 small onion, skinned and finely chopped* |
| *450 g (1 lb) ripe fresh tomatoes, skinned, seeded and chopped* |
| *1 garlic clove, skinned and crushed* |
| *about 150 ml (5 fl oz) vegetable stock or water* |
| *½ × 15 ml tbs tomato purée* |
| *pinch of caster sugar, or to taste* |
| *salt and pepper* |
| *1 × 15 ml tbs dry white wine* |

Aubergine Cannelloni

**1** Make the tomato sauce. Heat the olive oil in a heavy saucepan, add the onion and cook gently, stirring frequently, for 5 minutes. Add the tomatoes and garlic, cover and cook over gentle heat, stirring occasionally, for 10 minutes. Add the stock or water, tomato purée, sugar and salt and pepper to taste. Half-cover the pan and simmer for 30 minutes, stirring frequently.

**2** Remove the pan from the heat, then work the tomato mixture through a fine sieve into a clean saucepan. Bring to the boil, stirring, add the wine and set aside.

**3** Cut the aubergines lengthways into thin slices, discarding the ends and rounded pieces from the sides. Heat 2-3 × 15 ml tbs olive oil in a large non-stick frying pan. Add a single layer of aubergine slices and fry over moderate heat until light golden on both sides. Remove from the pan, drain, then place on absorbent kitchen paper. Repeat with more oil and the remaining aubergine slices.

**4** Put the ricotta and Parmesan cheeses in a bowl with the shredded basil and salt and pepper to taste. Beat well to mix.

**5** Place the aubergine slices on a clean work surface; if the slices are small or broken, overlap 2 slices so that they will roll up as one (you will need about 12 cannelloni altogether). Spoon the cheese mixture along the length of the aubergines, then roll the slices up around it.

**6** Place the rolls, seam-side down, in a single layer in an ovenproof dish. Bake in the oven at 190°C/375°F/Gas Mark 5 for 10-15 minutes or until hot. Meanwhile, reheat the tomato sauce until bubbling, taste and adjust seasoning, and add more stock or water if necessary.

**7** Arrange 3 cannelloni on each warmed plate. Drizzle the tomato sauce over, then sprinkle lightly with Parmesan and garnish with fresh basil leaves. Serve hot.

# CRESPELLINI

SERVES 4

*450 g (1 lb) washed fresh spinach, cooked, or 225 g (8 oz) frozen leaf spinach, thawed*

*50 g (2 oz) margarine or butter*

*1 small onion, skinned and finely chopped*

*65 g (2½ oz) freshly grated Parmesan cheese*

*600 ml (20 fl oz) Béchamel Sauce (see page 26)*

*PANCAKES*

*115 g (4 oz) plain flour*

*salt and pepper*

*1 egg*

*300 ml (10 fl oz) milk*

*vegetable oil, for frying*

**1** To make the pancake batter, place the flour and a pinch of salt in a bowl. Make a well in the centre and add the egg. Beat well with a wooden spoon and gradually stir in the milk.

**2** Heat a little oil in an 18 cm (7 in) heavy-based frying pan, tipping the pan to coat it evenly with oil, then pour in just enough batter to coat the base thinly. Fry for 1-2 minutes until golden brown, turn or toss and cook the second side. Repeat to make eight pancakes.

**3** Drain the spinach well and chop finely. Melt the margarine or butter in a saucepan, add the onion and fry gently for 5 minutes or until soft but not coloured. Stir in the spinach and cook for a further 2 minutes. Remove from the heat and stir in 50 g (2 oz) Parmesan cheese and 6 × 15 ml tbs Béchamel Sauce. Season with salt and pepper to taste.

**4** Spread an equal amount of the filling on each pancake, leaving a border around the edges. Roll up the pancakes loosely, and arrange them in a single layer in a buttered ovenproof dish.

**5** Pour the remaining Béchamel Sauce over and sprinkle with the remaining Parmesan cheese. Bake in the oven at 220°C/425°F/Gas Mark 7 for 15-20 minutes or until golden brown.

# ROCKET AND MELON SALAD WITH PROSCIUTTO

SERVES 4

*115 g (4 oz) rocket or baby spinach leaves*

*¼-½ cantaloupe melon, quartered, skinned and seeded*

*8 slices prosciutto, each torn in half*

*25 g (1 oz) piece of Parmesan cheese*

*6 × 15 ml tbs extra-virgin olive oil*

*2 × 15 ml tbs balsamic or white wine vinegar*

*4 sun-dried tomatoes in oil, drained and finely chopped*

*salt and pepper*

**1** Arrange the rocket or spinach leaves on four individual plates. Cut the melon into thin slices and arrange on the rocket with the prosciutto.

**2** Using a potato peeler, pare thin shavings of Parmesan and scatter over the salad. Just before serving, whisk together the olive oil and vinegar. Stir in the chopped sun-dried tomatoes and season with salt and pepper to taste. Drizzle the tomato dressing over the salad.

COOK'S TIP

Rocket is a leafy salad vegetable native to the Mediterranean. It has ragged, dandelion-shaped leaves with a slightly hot, peppery flavour. When unavailable use tender young spinach leaves or watercress instead.

*Crespellini*

# POTATO GNOCCHI

SERVES 4

*900 g (2 lb) old floury potatoes, such as King Edward
or Maris Piper*

*salt*

*50 g (2 oz) margarine or butter*

*1 egg, beaten*

*225-275 g (8-10 oz) plain flour*

*1 jar of fresh pesto sauce*

*freshly grated Parmesan cheese, to serve (optional)*

**1** Cook the potatoes in their skins in boiling salted water for about 20 minutes or until tender. Drain well, cool slightly and peel. While the potatoes are still warm, push them through a sieve into a large bowl. Add $1 \times 5$ ml tsp salt, the margarine or butter, egg and half the flour. Mix well to bind together.

**2** Turn the mixture out on to a floured surface and knead, gradually adding more flour, until dough is soft, smooth and slightly sticky.

**3** With floured hands, roll the dough into 2.5 cm (1 in) thick ropes. Cut the ropes into 2 cm (¾ in) pieces.

**4** Press a finger into each piece of dough to flatten, then draw your finger towards you to curl the sides of the gnocchi. Alternatively, make a decorative shape by using the same rolling technique, but roll each gnocchi over the end of the prongs of a fork. Spread the gnocchi out on a floured tea-towel.

**5** Bring a large pan of salted water to the boil and reduce to barely simmering. Drop in a few gnocchi at a time and cook gently for 2-3 minutes or until they float to the surface.

**6** With a slotted spoon, remove the gnocchi from the pan, then place them in a greased serving dish. Cover and keep warm while cooking the remaining gnocchi.

**7** When all the gnocchi are cooked, toss them in pesto sauce. Serve immediately, sprinkled with Parmesan, if using.

# SPINACH GNOCCHI

SERVES 4

*900 g (2 lb) fresh spinach, washed or 450 g (1 lb)
frozen spinach*

*225 g (8 oz) curd cheese*

*2 eggs, beaten*

*225 g (8 oz) plain flour*

*¼ × 5 ml tsp freshly grated nutmeg*

*115 g (4 oz) freshly grated Parmesan cheese*

*salt and pepper*

*115 g (4 oz) margarine or butter*

**1** Place the spinach in a saucepan without any water, cover and cook gently for 5-10 minutes or until tender, or thaw if using frozen spinach. Drain well and chop finely.

**2** Mix together the curd cheese, eggs, flour, spinach, nutmeg and half the Parmesan. Season with salt and pepper. With floured hands, form the mixture into cork-sized croquettes, or balls the size of large marbles. Chill in the refrigerator for at least 1 hour.

**3** Bring a large pan of salted water to the boil and reduce to barely simmering. Drop in a few gnocchi at a time and cook for 8-10 minutes or until they float to the surface. With a slotted spoon, remove the gnocchi from the pan and place in a greased serving dish. Cover and keep warm while cooking the remaining gnocchi in the same way.

**4** Melt the margarine or butter in a small saucepan and pour it over the gnocchi. Sprinkle with the remaining cheese and serve immediately.

LEFT Spinach Gnocchi
RIGHT Potato Gnocchi

# PASTA
# AND RICE

*In this chapter you will find a varied selection of pasta
and rice dishes, some suited to family meals, others more
elaborate and stylish for special occasions. Pasta – that most
Italian of all foods – can be served in so many delectable
ways (with different meats, fish, vegetables and sauces) to give
infinite variety. In Italy, pasta is even served as a starter. Rice,
too, blends happily with other ingredients to give deliciously
tasty dishes, such as the famous Italian speciality, risotto.*

OPPOSITE
LEFT Asparagus Risotto
RIGHT Beef Cannelloni

# PASTA BAKE

SERVES 3–4

| |
|---|
| 75 g (3 oz) Gruyère cheese, grated |
| ¼ × 5 ml tsp freshly grated nutmeg |
| salt and pepper |
| 225 g (8 oz) dried conchiglie or farfalle |
| 1½ × Tomato Sauce (see page 19) |
| 4 × 15 ml tbs freshly grated Parmesan cheese |
| 3 × 15 ml tbs dried breadcrumbs |
| BÉCHAMEL SAUCE |
| 300 ml (10 fl oz) milk |
| 1 bay leaf |
| 25 g (1 oz) butter |
| 25 g (1 oz) plain flour |

1 To make the Béchamel Sauce, put the milk and bay leaf in a saucepan and slowly bring to the boil. Remove from the heat. Melt the butter in a separate saucepan. Sprinkle in the flour and cook over a low heat for 1-2 minutes, stirring. Remove from the heat.

2 Discard the bay leaf from the milk. Gradually blend the milk into the mixture, stirring well.

3 Bring to the boil slowly and cook, stirring, until the sauce thickens. Simmer very gently for a further 2-3 minutes, then add the cheese and nutmeg, season with salt and pepper and stir until the cheese has melted.

4 Cook the pasta in boiling salted water for about 10 minutes or until *al dente* (tender but slightly firm). Drain the pasta and mix with the Tomato Sauce. Spread half this mixture in the bottom of a buttered ovenproof dish and cover with half the Béchamel Sauce. Repeat the layers, then sprinkle with the Parmesan and breadcrumbs.

5 Bake in the oven at 190°C/375°F/Gas Mark 5 for 20 minutes, then brown under a hot grill for 5 minutes. Serve immediately.

# BEEF CANNELLONI

SERVES 4–6

| |
|---|
| 15 g (½ oz) butter |
| 2 × 15 ml tbs vegetable oil |
| 1 onion, skinned and chopped |
| 50 g (2 oz) smoked streaky bacon, rinded and chopped |
| 335 g (12 oz) lean minced beef |
| 1 × 15 ml tbs tomato purée |
| 150 ml (5 fl oz) red wine |
| 2 egg yolks |
| pinch of freshly grated nutmeg |
| 225 g (8 oz) ricotta or curd cheese |
| 50 g (2 oz) freshly grated Parmesan cheese |
| salt and pepper |
| 1.2 lt (2 pt) Béchamel Sauce (see left) |
| 12-18 tubes oven-ready cannelloni |
| parsley sprigs, to garnish |

1 Melt the butter and oil in a medium, heavy-based saucepan, add the onion and fry for 5 minutes until soft but not coloured. Add the bacon and cook for 2 minutes.

2 Add the beef, increase the heat and cook until well browned, removing any lumps with a fork. Stir in the tomato purée and red wine. Cook, stirring, until most of the liquid has evaporated. Set aside to cool for 10 minutes.

3 Mix together the meat, egg yolks, nutmeg, ricotta, 25 g (1 oz) Parmesan and seasoning. Pour half of the Béchamel Sauce into a shallow ovenproof dish large enough to take the cannelloni in a single layer.

4 With a spoon, fill the cannelloni with the meat. Lay them side by side in the dish. Coat with the remaining Béchamel Sauce, sprinkle the remaining cheese on top and bake at 200°C/400°F/Gas Mark 6 for 20 minutes. Garnish with parsley before serving.

Pasta Bake

# SPAGHETTI WITH GARLIC

SERVES 6

---
*450 g (1 lb) dried spaghetti*
---
*salt and pepper*
---
*5 × 15 ml tbs virgin olive oil*
---
*2 garlic cloves, skinned and crushed*
---
*1 fresh chilli, seeded and chopped*
---
*2 × 15 ml tbs chopped fresh parsley, coriander or basil (optional)*
---

**1** Cook the spaghetti in boiling salted water for 8-10 minutes or until *al dente* (tender but slightly firm).

**2** Meanwhile, heat the oil in a heavy-based saucepan, add the garlic and chilli and fry for 3-4 minutes, stirring occasionally. Do not allow the garlic and chilli to become too brown or the oil will taste bitter. Remove from the heat and set aside until the pasta is cooked.

**3** Drain the pasta thoroughly. Reheat the oil over a very high heat for 1 minute, then pour over the pasta with the herbs, if using. Season with salt and pepper to taste and serve immediately.

# TAGLIATELLE WITH TOMATO SAUCE

SERVES 4–6

---
*2 × 15 ml tbs olive oil*
---
*1 small onion, skinned and finely chopped*
---
*2 celery sticks, trimmed and finely chopped*
---
*2 carrots, peeled and finely chopped*
---
*2 garlic cloves, skinned and crushed*
---
*2 × 400 g cans chopped tomatoes*
---
*2 × 15 ml tbs tomato purée*
---
*150 ml (5 fl oz) dry white wine*
---
*salt and pepper*
---
*450-675 g (1-1½ lb) dried tagliatelle*
---

**1** Heat the oil in a large saucepan. Add the onion, celery and carrot and cook, stirring, for 8-10 minutes or until beginning to soften.

**2** Stir in the garlic, canned tomatoes, tomato purée and wine. Season to taste with salt and pepper, cover and simmer for about 30 minutes, stirring occasionally.

**3** Meanwhile, cook the tagliatelle in boiling salted water for 8-10 minutes or until *al dente* (tender but slightly firm).

4 Pour about half the sauce into a blender or food processor and work until smooth. Stir into the remaining sauce and reheat.

**5** Drain the tagliatelle and transfer to a serving bowl. Pour the sauce over the pasta and serve immediately.

Spaghetti with Garlic

# LAMB AND SPINACH LASAGNE

Lamb and Spinach Lasagne

SERVES 6

*450 g (1 lb) fresh spinach, washed, or 225 g (8 oz)*
*frozen spinach*

*2 × 15 ml tbs vegetable oil*

*1 onion, skinned and chopped*

*450 g (1 lb) minced lamb*

*227 g can tomatoes*

*1 garlic clove, skinned and crushed*

*2 × 15 ml tbs chopped fresh mint*

*1 × 5 ml tsp ground cinnamon*

*freshly grated nutmeg*

*salt and pepper*

*50 g (2 oz) butter or margarine*

*50 g (2 oz) plain flour*

*900 ml (1½ pt) milk*

*150 ml (5 fl oz) natural yogurt*

*12-15 sheets pre-cooked lasagne*

*175 g (6 oz) Cheddar cheese, grated*

*tomato and chive salad, to serve*

**1** Place the spinach in a saucepan without any water, cover and cook gently for about 4 min-utes or until tender, or thaw if using frozen spinach. Drain well and chop finely.

**2** Heat the oil in a large saucepan, add the onion and fry gently for 5 minutes. Add the lamb and brown well, then drain off all the fat.

**3** Stir in the spinach with the tomatoes and their juice, the garlic, mint and cinnamon. Season with nutmeg, salt and pepper to taste. Bring to the boil and simmer, uncovered, for about 30 minutes. Leave to cool while making the sauce.

**4** Melt the butter in a saucepan, add the flour and cook gently, stirring, for 1-2 minutes. Remove from the heat and gradually blend in the milk. Bring to the boil, stirring, constantly, then simmer for 3 minutes until thick and smooth. Add the yogurt and salt and pepper to taste.

**5** Spoon one-third of the meat mixture over the base of a rectangular baking dish. Cover with 4-5 sheets of lasagne and spread one-third of the white sauce over. Repeat these layers twice more, finishing with the sauce. Sprinkle the cheese on top.

**6** Stand the dish on a baking tray. Bake in the oven at 180°C/350°F/Gas Mark 4 for 45-50 minutes, or until the top is well browned.

# CAPELLETTI WITH RICOTTA AND PRAWNS

SERVES 4

| |
|---|
| 225 g (8 oz) plain flour |
| 2 × size 3 eggs |
| 150 g (5 oz) frozen chopped spinach, thawed and squeezed dry |
| cooked prawns and parsley sprigs, to garnish |
| FILLING |
| 2 × 15 ml tbs olive oil |
| 1 shallot, skinned and finely chopped |
| 1 garlic clove, skinned and crushed |
| 115 g (4 oz) button mushrooms, wiped and chopped |
| 175 g (6 oz) ricotta cheese |
| 2 × size 3 egg yolks |
| 115 g (4 oz) cooked peeled prawns, chopped |
| 4 × 15 ml tbs chopped fresh parsley |
| salt and pepper |
| SAUCE |
| 6 × 15 ml tbs double cream |
| 3 × 15 ml tbs melted butter |
| 40 g (1½ oz) freshly grated Parmesan cheese |

1 To make the filling, heat the oil in a saucepan and cook the shallot gently for 5 minutes. Add the garlic and mushrooms and cook for 2-3 minutes.

2 Remove the pan from the heat and stir in the ricotta, egg yolks, prawns and parsley and season with salt and pepper. Set aside.

3 To make the pasta, heap the flour on a work surface and make a well in the centre. Break the eggs into the well and add the spinach. Work the flour into the eggs and spinach with your fingers to form a dough. Knead the dough lightly for about 5 minutes.

4 Cover with a tea-towel and leave to rest for 15 minutes, then roll out thinly on a floured work surface. Cut into 9 cm (3½ in) squares.

5 Dampen the edges of the squares, and place about 1 × 15 ml tbs filling on each. Fold the squares in half to form triangles and press edges to seal. Wrap the capelletti around one finger, dampen the corners and press together. Leave to dry on a tea-towel.

6 Cook the capelletti in a large pan of boiling salted water for 10-12 minutes, or until *al dente* (tender but slightly firm). Meanwhile, make the sauce, heat the cream and butter in a saucepan for 2-3 minutes, add half the Parmesan and simmer for 1 minute. Drain the capelletti. Pour the sauce over, sprinkle with the remaining Parmesan and garnish with prawns and parsley.

# PENNE WITH CHICKEN AND CHERRY TOMATOES

SERVES 4

| |
|---|
| 335 g (12 oz) dried penne rigate pasta |
| salt and pepper |
| 2 × 15 ml tbs olive oil |
| 3 boneless chicken breasts, skinned and cut into cubes |
| 335 g (12 oz) cherry tomatoes, halved |
| 1 garlic clove, skinned and crushed |
| 1 jar of fresh pesto sauce |

1 Cook the penne in a large saucepan of boiling salted water for 10-12 minutes, or until *al dente* (tender but slightly firm). Meanwhile, heat the oil in a frying pan, add the chicken and cook for 6-8 minutes until browned.

2 Add the tomatoes and garlic to the frying pan and cook for 2-3 minutes until beginning to soften, then stir in the pesto. Add pepper to taste and heat through.

3 Drain the penne thoroughly and tip into the pan with the chicken. Toss lightly and serve.

FRONT Capelletti with Ricotta and Prawns
BACK Penne with Chicken and Cherry Tomatoes

# RAVIOLI WITH MUSSEL SAUCE

### SERVES 4

| |
|---|
| *200 g (7 oz) plain flour* |
| *2 × size 3 eggs* |
| *3 × 15 ml tbs tomato purée* |
| *a few shredded basil leaves, to garnish* |
| *FILLING* |
| *1 shallot, skinned and finely chopped* |
| *1 celery stick, trimmed and finely chopped* |
| *1 small carrot, peeled and finely chopped* |
| *225 g (8 oz) haddock fillet* |
| *3 × 15 ml tbs white wine* |
| *150 ml (5 fl oz) water* |
| *1 egg yolk* |
| *2 × 15 ml tbs grated Parmesan cheese* |
| *1 × 15 ml tbs chopped fresh parsley* |
| *a little grated nutmeg* |
| *salt and pepper* |
| *SAUCE* |
| *3 × 15 ml tbs olive oil* |
| *2 garlic cloves, skinned and crushed* |
| *2 × 15 ml tbs drained, finely chopped sun-dried tomatoes in oil* |
| *6 × 15 ml tbs dry white wine* |
| *225 g (8 oz) cooked, shelled mussels* |
| *150 ml (5 fl oz) double cream* |

1 Make the filling, place the vegetables in a shallow frying pan, lay the fish on top and add the wine and water. Simmer for 10-15 minutes.

2 Lift out the fish and remove any skin and bones. Place the fish, egg yolk, Parmesan and parsley in a food processor and process until smooth. Season with nutmeg, salt and pepper.

3 To make the pasta, heap the flour on a work surface and make a well in the centre. Break the eggs into the well and add the tomato purée. Work the flour into the eggs and tomato purée with your fingers to form a dough. Knead the dough lightly for about 5 minutes.

4 Cover with a tea-towel and leave to rest for

15 minutes. Roll out the pasta on a floured board to a 30 × 60 cm (12 × 24 in) rectangle and cut in half. Spoon small mounds of filling, evenly spaced at 5 cm (2 in) intervals, on to one sheet of pasta. Brush water around the mounds of filling, then lay the second sheet on top. Press down the pasta around the mounds of filling to seal, then cut into rounds using a 5 cm (2 in) cutter.

5 Cook the pasta in boiling salted water for 3-5 minutes, or until *al dente* (tender but slightly firm). Make the sauce, heat the oil in a saucepan and add the garlic, tomatoes and wine and simmer for 2-3 minutes. Add the mussels and cream and heat through gently.

6 Drain the pasta and pour the sauce over. Garnish with shredded basil and serve at once.

# THREE CHEESE PASTA

### SERVES 4

| |
|---|
| *335 g (12 oz) fresh white spaghetti* |
| *salt* |
| *40 g (1½ oz) unsalted butter* |
| *75 g (3 oz) dolcelatte, cut into small cubes* |
| *175 g (6 oz) mascarpone cheese* |
| *75 g (3 oz) Parmesan cheese, grated* |
| *40 g (1½ oz) walnuts, chopped* |
| *1 × 15 ml tbs snipped chives* |

1 Cook the pasta in boiling salted water for 3-5 minutes, until *al dente* (tender but slightly firm). Meanwhile, melt the butter in a pan, add the dolcelatte and mascarpone cheeses and heat gently until melted.

2 Drain the pasta thoroughly and stir in the melted cheese mixture. Scatter the Parmesan, walnuts and chives over the top, toss and serve.

LEFT Ravioli with Mussel Sauce
RIGHT Three Cheese Pasta

# TIMBALLO

SERVES 8

| |
|---|
| 75 g (3 oz) margarine or butter |
| 1 onion, skinned and finely chopped |
| 400 g (14 oz) arborio rice |
| 180 ml (6½ fl oz) dry white wine |
| about 1.1 lt (2 pt) hot vegetable stock |
| salt and pepper |
| 2 × 15 ml tbs olive oil |
| 225 g (8 oz) mushrooms, wiped and sliced |
| 2 garlic cloves, skinned and crushed |
| 2 × 5 ml tsp chopped fresh basil or 1 × 5 ml tsp dried |
| 4 × 15 ml tbs dried breadcrumbs |
| 50 g (2 oz) freshly grated Parmesan cheese |
| 2 eggs, beaten |
| 3 hard-boiled eggs, shelled and sliced |
| 225 g (8 oz) Mozzarella cheese, sliced |
| fresh basil leaves and tomato slices, to garnish |
| tomato sauce, to serve |

1  First make the risotto. Melt 50 g (2 oz) of the margarine or butter in a heavy-based saucepan. Add the onion and fry gently for 5 minutes or until soft but not coloured. Add the rice and stir until coated in the fat, then pour in 150 ml (5 fl oz) of the wine and bring to the boil. Simmer, stirring until the liquid has been absorbed.

2  Pour in about 150 ml (5 fl oz) stock, add 1 × 5 ml tsp salt and simmer and stir as before until all the liquid is absorbed. Continue adding stock in this way until the rice is tender; this should take 15-20 minutes.

3  Meanwhile, heat the oil in a separate pan, add the mushrooms and garlic and fry gently until the juices run. Stir in the remaining wine and the basil. Season and remove from heat.

4  Sprinkle the breadcrumbs over the base and up the sides of a well-buttered 20 cm (8 in) spring-release cake tin or mould. Remove the risotto from the heat and stir in the Parmesan cheese with the beaten eggs, the remaining margarine or butter and salt and pepper to taste.

5  Press three-quarters of the risotto over the base and sides of tin. Arrange one-third of the egg slices in the bottom, sprinkle over one-third mushrooms and top with one-third of the cheese slices.

6  Repeat these layers using up the eggs, mushrooms and Mozzarella. Press the remaining risotto firmly on top. Cover the tin with foil and bake in the oven at 190°C/375°F/Gas Mark 5 for 1 hour or until firm. Leave for 5 minutes, before turning out. Garnish with basil leaves and tomato slices. Serve with tomato sauce.

# ASPARAGUS RISOTTO

SERVES 8

| |
|---|
| 2.1 lt (3½ pt) vegetable stock |
| 300 ml (10 fl oz) dry white wine |
| 900 g (2 lb) thin green asparagus |
| 175 g (6 oz) butter |
| 1 onion, skinned and finely chopped |
| 675 g (1½ lb) arborio rice |
| pinch of saffron powder |
| salt and pepper |
| 115 g (4 oz) freshly grated Parmesan cheese |

1  Heat stock and wine to barely simmering point. Cut off asparagus tips, peel the remainder and cut into short lengths.

2  In a large saucepan, melt 50 g (2 oz) butter, and fry the onion until soft. Add asparagus stems and rice and stir well.

3  Add a ladleful of stock to the pan, cook gently, stirring occasionally until the stock is absorbed. Stir in more stock as soon as each ladleful is absorbed.

4  Add the saffron and seasoning. Continue adding stock and stirring until the risotto is thick, creamy and tender. This takes 20-25 minutes.

5  Meanwhile, steam asparagus tips until tender, then stir into the risotto with remaining butter and the cheese.

Timballo

# CHICKEN AND VEGETABLE RISOTTO

SERVES 4

| |
|---|
| 175 g (6 oz) brown rice |
| 350 ml (12 fl oz) chicken stock |
| 50 g (2 oz) butter or margarine |
| 4 chicken quarters, halved, about 900 g (2 lb) total weight |
| 175 g (6 oz) carrots, peeled and cut into thick matchsticks |
| 225 g (8 oz) turnips, peeled and cut into thick matchsticks |
| 2 onions, skinned and chopped |
| 1 stick of celery, chopped |
| 50 g (2 oz) lean streaky bacon, rinded and diced |
| salt and pepper |
| 6 × 15 ml tbs dry white wine |
| chopped fresh parsley, to garnish |

**1** In a large saucepan, combine the rice and stock. Bring to the boil, then cover the pan and simmer for 15 minutes.
**2** Melt 25 g (1 oz) butter or margarine in a flameproof casserole. Add the chicken portions and fry for about 10 minutes until browned. Remove from the pan.
**3** Melt the remaining butter or margarine in the casserole, add all the vegetables and cook for 5 minutes until brown. Add the bacon and fry gently for a further 2 minutes.
**4** Stir in the rice mixture and season well. Arrange the chicken portions on top of the rice and vegetables. Spoon over the white wine.
**5** Cover the casserole tightly with the lid or foil, then bake in the oven at 180°C/350°F/Gas Mark 4 for about 1 hour until the chicken is tender.
**6** Just before serving, fork up the rice and vegetables round the chicken. Taste and adjust seasoning, then serve, garnished with parsley.

# TOASTED POLENTA

SERVES 6

| |
|---|
| 200 g (7 oz) polenta |
| 1.1 lt (2 pt) cold water |
| 1 × 5 ml tsp salt |
| 25 g (1 oz) butter |
| 1 garlic clove, skinned and crushed |
| pepper |

**1** Place the polenta in a saucepan with the cold water. Add the salt and simmer for about 15 minutes until really thick and no longer grainy. Stir frequently to prevent sticking. Remove from the heat and stir in the butter, garlic and pepper to taste.
**2** Turn out on to a wooden board or plate and spread to a thickness of about 1-2 cm (½-¾ in). Cool, cover and chill in the refrigerator for at least 1 hour. Cut into 5 cm (2 in) squares.
**3** Toast squares on both sides under a hot grill for 7-10 minutes. Serve at once or cover loosely and keep warm.

COOK'S TIP

Polenta is the Italian name for ground corn or maize and looks like a golden flour or semolina. An 'instant' polenta is also available (which cooks in 5 minutes) although lovers of polenta agree it is no substitute for the real thing.

Fried polenta instead of toasted is also delicious: follow the insructions above to the end of step 2, then deep-fry the polenta cubes in hot oil until crisp and golden. Drain well before serving.

TOP Toasted Polenta
BOTTOM Chicken and Vegetable Risotto

# PIZZAS

*Pizzas enjoy constant popularity – hardly surprising for good ones are surely one of the most delicious of foods. Find out, in the following recipes, just how easy it is to make a perfect yeast dough base in the true Italian tradition, and discover a selection of mouthwatering toppings. For a change, try shaping the dough differently, as in Panzerotti and Calzone – ideal for informal eating.*

OPPOSITE Four Seasons Pizza

# FOUR SEASONS PIZZA

MAKES 4

### BASIC PIZZA DOUGH

| |
|---|
| 450 g (1 lb) strong white or wholemeal flour |
| 1 × 5 ml tsp fast-action dried yeast |
| 1 × 5 ml tsp salt |
| 300 ml (10 fl oz) tepid water |
| 2 × 15 ml tbs olive oil |

### TOPPING

| |
|---|
| 3 × 15 ml tbs olive oil |
| 175 g (6 oz) button mushrooms, wiped and sliced |
| 2 garlic cloves, skinned and crushed |
| 2 × 5 ml tsp chopped fresh basil or 1 × 5 ml tsp dried basil |
| 1 quantity Tomato Sauce (see page 19) |
| 16 slices of Italian salami, rinded |
| 50 g (2 oz) black olives |
| 400 g can artichoke hearts, drained and sliced |
| 225 g (8 oz) Italian Mozzarella cheese, thinly sliced |
| 4 tomatoes, skinned and sliced |
| 1 × 5 ml tsp dried oregano |
| salt and pepper |
| fresh oregano leaves, to garnish |

**1** To make the Basic Pizza Dough, put the flour, yeast and the salt in a bowl and mix together. Make a well in the centre and add the tepid water and the olive oil. Beat well until the dough leaves the side of the bowl clean. Add a little more tepid water if necessary. Turn on to a lightly floured surface and knead for 10 minutes until smooth and elastic.

**2** Heat 2 × 15 ml tbs oil in a pan, add the mushrooms, garlic and basil and fry for 2-3 minutes. Roll out the dough and cut into four 20 cm (8 in) circles. Make the edges slightly thicker than the centres. Put the circles of dough into oiled sandwich tins. Spread the Tomato Sauce over dough.

**3** Cut each slice of salami into four quarters. Arrange these pieces in one quarter of each pizza, overlapping them to cover tomato sauce. Dot with olives. Arrange the artichoke slices over another quarter, the cheese and tomato over another and mushrooms over the last.

**4** Sprinkle the remaining oil over the pizzas with the oregano and seasoning. Leave the pizzas to prove in a warm place for about 30 minutes, then bake in the oven at 220°C/425°F/Gas Mark 7 for 25 minutes swapping the pizzas around halfway through the cooking time. Serve garnished with oregano.

# PANZEROTTI

MAKES 16

| |
|---|
| 1 quantity Basic Pizza Dough (see left) |
| Tomato Sauce (see page 19) or tomato purée |
| about 175 g (6 oz) Mozzarella or goats' cheese, chopped |
| salt and pepper |
| vegetable oil for deep-frying |
| Pesto Sauce or Tomato Sauce, to serve |

**1** Make the Basic Pizza Dough following the instructions (see left) and leave in a warm place to rise. Turn the risen dough out on to a floured surface, knead lightly and divide into 16 equal pieces. Using a rolling pin, roll each to a circle measuring 10 cm (4 in) in diameter.

**2** Spread only 1 × 5 ml tsp Tomato Sauce or purée on to each circle, leaving a border around the edge. Sprinkle the cheese over the tomato and season with salt and pepper.

**3** Brush the edges with water, then fold in half to enclose the filling. Press the edges firmly, then crimp to seal in the filling. Make sure that you do this thoroughly.

**4** Half-fill a deep-fat fryer with oil and heat to 180°C/350°F or until a cube of day-old bread browns in 1 minute. Deep-fry the panzerotti in batches for 2-3 minutes or until golden brown. Drain on absorbent kitchen paper, and serve hot, topped with Pesto or Tomato Sauce.

Panzerotti

# FARMHOUSE PIZZA

SERVES 6

*1 quantity Basic Pizza Dough (see page 40)*

*4 × 15 ml tbs olive oil*

*2 garlic cloves, skinned and crushed*

*225 g (8 oz) button mushrooms, wiped*

*400 g can tomatoes*

*salt and pepper*

*400 g (14 oz) Italian Mozzarella cheese, thinly sliced*

*115 g (4 oz) boiled ham, cut into strips*

*50 g (2 oz) bottled mussels or can anchovy fillets, drained*

*10 black olives, halved and stoned*

*4 × 5 ml tsp chopped fresh oregano or 2 × 5 ml tsp dried oregano*

*fresh oregano leaves, to garnish*

**1** Make the Basic Pizza Dough following the instructions on page 40.

**2** Heat 2 × 15 ml tbs oil in a heavy-based frying pan and fry the garlic and mushrooms for 5 minutes.

**3** Turn the dough on to a floured surface and roll out to a 30 × 25 cm (12 × 10 in) rectangle. Make the edges slightly thicker than the centre. Put the dough on an oiled baking tray.

**4** Mash the tomatoes with half of their juice and spread over the dough. Sprinkle with salt and pepper to taste.

**5** Arrange the slices of Mozzarella over the tomatoes, then sprinkle the strips of ham over. Top with the mushrooms and mussels or anchovies, then dot with the olives. Mix together the oregano and remaining oil, and add salt and pepper to taste. Drizzle over the top of the pizza.

**6** Leave the pizza to prove in a warm place for about 30 minutes, then bake in the oven at 220°C/425°F/Gas Mark 7 for 25 minutes or until the topping is melted and the dough well risen. Cut into portions and serve hot or cold, garnished with oregano.

# CALZONE

MAKES 4

*450 g (1 lb) strong white flour*

*1 sachet fast-action dried yeast*

*1 × 5 ml tsp salt*

*350 ml (12 fl oz) tepid water*

*1 × 15 ml tbs olive oil*

**FILLING**

*300 ml (10 fl oz) Tomato Sauce (see page 19)*

*225 g (8 oz) sliced pepperoni sausage*

*150 g (5 oz) Italian Mozzarella cheese, diced*

*4 × 15 ml tbs shredded fresh basil*

*pepper*

*4 eggs*

*flat-leaved parsley sprigs, to garnish*

**1** Sift the flour into a large bowl and stir in the yeast and salt. Make a well in the centre, add the tepid water and olive oil and mix to a soft dough. Turn the dough on to a lightly floured surface and knead for about 10 minutes until smooth and elastic. Place the dough in an oiled bowl, cover with a tea-towel and leave to rise in a warm place for 30 minutes.

**2** Knock back the dough, by punching it once or twice, then tip out on to a lightly floured surface and knead for a few minutes until smooth. Divide the dough into four equal pieces and roll out to 25 cm (10 in) rounds.

**3** Spread the Tomato Sauce over half of each round. Scatter a quarter of the pepperoni and cheese over the sauce on each round. Sprinkle with the basil and black pepper, then dampen the edges of the dough. Make an indentation in each filling, then break an egg into each indentation. Fold over the dough to make a semi-circle and press the edges to seal.

**4** Lift the calzone on to two greased baking trays and cook near the top of the oven at 230°C/450°F/Gas Mark 8 for 10-12 minutes until well browned. Serve at once, garnished with parsley sprigs

LEFT Farmhouse Pizza
RIGHT Calzone

# MEAT AND
# FISH DISHES

*Just a glance through the following pages shows how wonderfully varied Italian main courses can be using a combination of fresh flavours and quality ingredients, cooked simply, but with style. The recipes range from succulent roast chicken with fennel, or piquant flash-fried steak with garlic, herbs and tomatoes, to a fabulous dish of trout fillets baked over garlicky potatoes.*

OPPOSITE
LEFT Beef with Mushrooms and Sweet Peppers
RIGHT Chicken with Rosemary

# CHICKEN CACCIATORA

SERVES 4

| 25 g (1 oz) butter |
| 2 × 15 ml tbs olive oil |
| 4 chicken portions |
| 1 onion, skinned and chopped |
| 2 garlic cloves, skinned and crushed |
| 225 g (8 oz) button mushrooms, wiped and sliced |
| 150 ml (5 fl oz) dry white wine |
| 400 g can tomatoes, drained |
| 2 × 5 ml tsp dried mixed herbs |
| 1 × 5 ml tsp dried oregano |
| salt and pepper |

1  Melt the butter with the oil in a large flame-proof casserole. Add the chicken and fry over moderate heat for 5-10 minutes until well coloured on all sides. Remove from the pan with a slotted spoon and drain on absorbent kitchen paper.

2  Add the onion and garlic to the pan and fry gently until soft. Return the chicken to the pan, add the mushrooms and wine and simmer for 10 minutes.

3  Add the tomatoes, herbs and salt and pepper to taste, then cover and simmer for a further 35 minutes or until the chicken is tender. Taste and adjust seasoning before serving.

COOK'S TIP

For added interest and flavour, use a mixture of mushrooms in this dish such as oyster and shiitake. These varieties of mushroom are now increasingly available and are particularly good in chicken dishes and with shellfish.

# CHICKEN WITH ROSEMARY

SERVES 4

| 2 × 15 ml tbs white wine vinegar |
| 1 × 15 ml tbs water |
| 7.5 cm (3 in) sprig of rosemary, chopped |
| salt and pepper |
| 4 chicken leg joints |
| 2 × 15 ml tbs olive oil |
| lemon wedges and fresh rosemary sprigs, to garnish |

1  Put the vinegar into a glass, add the water, rosemary and salt and pepper to taste. Stir well, then leave to infuse while cooking the chicken.

2  Season the chicken pieces with salt and pepper. Heat the oil in a large frying pan and, when hot, add the chicken pieces and fry for 5 minutes until just golden brown on all sides. Lower the heat and cook uncovered for about 35 minutes.

3  Using two slotted spoons, turn the chicken frequently during cooking until the skin is brown and crisp and the juices run clear when the flesh is pierced with a fork.

4  Remove the pan from the heat. When the fat has stopped sizzling, pour over the wine vinegar infusion. Return to the heat, boil rapidly to reduce the liquid for about 5 minutes, then serve immediately, garnished with lemon wedges and sprigs of rosemary.

COOK'S TIP

Rosemary is a pungent herb with spiky leaves. Since the leaves can be tough, it is advisable to chop them before adding to a dish cooking. Fresh sprigs make an attractive garnish.

Chicken Cacciatora

# FENNEL-STUFFED ROAST CHICKEN

SERVES 4–6

| |
|---|
| 1.8 kg (4 lb) oven-ready chicken |
| 4 × 15 ml tbs vegetable oil |
| 1 small onion, skinned and finely chopped |
| 1 garlic clove, skinned and crushed |
| 1 small bulb of fennel |
| 4 rashers smoked streaky bacon, diced |
| 115 g (4 oz) fresh white breadcrumbs |
| 25 g (1 oz) freshly grated Parmesan cheese |
| 1 egg, beaten |
| salt and pepper |
| 25 g (1 oz) butter |
| 150 ml (5 fl oz) dry white wine |

**1** Make the stuffing. Heat half the oil in a small pan, add the onion and garlic and fry gently for 5 minutes until soft but not coloured. Chop the fennel finely, reserving the feathery tops for the garnish.

**2** Add the fennel to the onion and continue frying for 5 minutes, stirring constantly. Add the bacon and fry for a further 5 minutes until changing colour.

**3** Transfer the fried mixture to a bowl. Add the breadcrumbs, Parmesan, egg and salt and pepper to taste. Mix well to combine. Fill the neck end of the chicken with the stuffing, then truss with string.

**4** Heat the remaining oil with the butter in a large flameproof casserole, then brown the chicken lightly on all sides. Turn the chicken the right way up, pour in the wine and bring to boiling point. Add salt and pepper to taste.

**5** Transfer the casserole to the oven and cook the chicken at 180°C/350°F/Gas Mark 4 for 1¾ hours, or until the juices run clear when the thickest part of the thigh is pierced with a skewer. Turn the chicken frequently during cooking.

**6** Remove the trussing string and carve the chicken into neat slices. Garnish each serving with a little of the reserved fennel tops. Hand the cooking liquid separately, if liked, or make a gravy in the usual way.

# PAN-FRIED CHICKEN WITH YELLOW PEPPERS AND CARROT

SERVES 4

| |
|---|
| 4 boneless chicken breasts, skinned |
| 3 × 15 ml tbs olive oil |
| ½ onion, skinned and finely sliced |
| 2 garlic cloves, skinned and crushed |
| 2 yellow peppers, seeded and sliced |
| 2 carrots, peeled and cut into matchsticks |
| 2 sticks celery, sliced diagonally |
| 4 plum tomatoes, quartered |
| salt and pepper |
| 150 ml (5 fl oz) dry white wine |

**1** Slash each chicken breast two or three times with a sharp knife. Heat the oil in a large frying pan, add the chicken and fry for 5-8 minutes, turning frequently until evenly browned. Add the onion, garlic, peppers, carrot, celery and tomatoes. Season with salt and pepper, then cover the pan and cook for 5 minutes.

**2** Pour in the wine and cook for over moderate heat for 10-15 minutes until the chicken is tender and the juices are reduced. Adjust the seasoning and serve hot.

TOP Fennel-stuffed Roast Chicken
BOTTOM Pan-fried Chicken with Yellow Peppers and Carrot

# BEEF WITH MUSHROOMS AND SWEET PEPPERS

### SERVES 8

| |
|---|
| *1.4 kg (3 lb) trimmed fillet of beef* |
| *25 g (1 oz) dried mushrooms, soaked and drained* |
| *285 g (9½ oz) jar pepperoni (sliced red and yellow peppers in sunflower oil), drained* |
| *salt and pepper* |
| *335 g (12 oz) smoked streaky bacon* |
| *2 × 15 ml tbs extra-virgin olive oil* |
| *2 × 5 ml tsp plain flour* |
| *150 ml (5 fl oz) full-bodied Italian red wine* |
| *300 ml (10 fl oz) beef stock* |
| *2 × 15 ml tbs Marsala wine or redcurrant jelly* |
| *2 × 5 ml tsp dried mixed herbs* |
| *flat-leaved parsley sprigs, to garnish* |

**1** Cut a slit along the side of the fillet, keeping both ends attached. Open it out with your fingers a little, to make a pocket. Roughly chop the mushrooms; reserve half for the sauce. Mix the remainder with half of the pepperoni and use to fill the pocket. Grind black pepper over the meat, then wrap the bacon around the fillet to enclose it completely. Tie with string at regular intervals.

**2** Heat the oil in a large non-stick frying pan, add the meat and seal on all sides. Lift the fillet out of the oil, drain over the pan, then place on absorbent kitchen paper. Reserve the juices in the pan for making the sauce later.

**3** Roast the fillet in the oven at 190°C/375°F/ Gas Mark 5 for 45 minutes. Remove from the oven, cover with foil and leave to rest in a warm place for 10-15 minutes.

**4** Meanwhile, reheat the reserved juices in the frying pan, sprinkle in the flour and cook, stirring, over moderate heat for 2-3 minutes. Gradually stir in the red wine and the stock, then bring to the boil, stirring. Lower the heat, add the Marsala or redcurrant jelly, the herbs and salt and pepper to taste. Simmer until thickened, stirring all the time. Add the remaining pepperoni and mushrooms and heat through.

**5** Remove the string and carve the meat into neat slices and arrange them on a warmed serving platter. Remove the pepperoni and mushrooms from the sauce with a slotted spoon and use to garnish the meat. Spoon a little sauce over the meat to glaze, then garnish with parsley. Serve immediately, with the remaining sauce handed separately in a sauceboat

# PIZZAIOLA STEAK

### SERVES 4

| |
|---|
| *4 thin rump steaks* |
| *4 × 15 ml tbs olive oil* |
| *2 garlic cloves, skinned and crushed* |
| *salt and pepper* |
| *450 g (1 lb) firm red tomatoes, skinned and chopped* |
| *3 × 15 ml tbs chopped fresh basil* |
| *3 × 5 ml tsp chopped fresh parsley* |
| *basil sprigs, to garnish* |

**1** Heat the oil in a large frying pan, add the steaks and fry quickly over a high heat for 2-3 minutes until browned on both sides. Add the garlic and salt and pepper to taste and fry for 30 seconds.

**2** Add the tomatoes and herbs and cook for 3-5 minutes until the tomatoes are softened and the juices reduced. Adjust the seasoning and serve at once, garnished with basil sprigs.

Pizzaiola Steak

# SALTIMBOCCA

SERVES 4

| |
|---|
| 4 veal escalopes, each weighing about 115 g (4 oz) |
| 8 slices prosciutto |
| 16 sage leaves |
| salt and pepper |
| 2 × 15 ml tbs olive oil |
| 25 g (1 oz) butter |
| 175 g (6 oz) mushrooms, wiped and sliced |
| 300 ml (10 fl oz) dry white wine |

**1** Place a veal escalope between two sheets of cling film and beat out thinly using a rolling pin. Repeat with remaining escalopes. Cut the escalopes in half crossways.

**2** Lay a slice of prosciutto on top of each piece of veal. Arrange two sage leaves on each piece and season with salt and pepper. Roll up the veal and secure each roll with a cocktail stick.

**3** Heat the oil and butter in a frying pan until foaming and add the veal rolls. Fry for 3-5 minutes until well browned on all sides. Add the mushrooms to the pan and cook for 2-3 minutes.

**4** Pour in the wine, allow to bubble up for a minute or two, then cover the pan, reduce the heat, and cook for 8-10 minutes until the veal is tender and cooked. Remove the lid and cook uncovered for 1-2 minutes to reduce the sauce slightly, if necessary, then check the seasoning and serve at once. Remove the cocktail sticks before serving.

COOK'S TIP

Prosciutto (or Parma ham) is a classic dry-cured Italian ham. It is sold in paper-thin slices and may be eaten raw or cooked.

# PARMESAN VEAL

SERVES 4

| |
|---|
| 4 veal escalopes, each weighing about 115 g (4 oz) |
| salt and pepper |
| 1 egg, beaten |
| 50 g (2 oz) fresh breadcrumbs |
| 4 × 15 ml tbs grated Parmesan cheese |
| 2 × 15 ml tbs olive oil |
| 115 g (4 oz) Italian Mozzarella cheese, sliced |
| 4 tomatoes, sliced |

**1** Place a veal escalope between two sheets of cling film and beat out thinly using a rolling pin. Repeat with remaining escalopes and season with salt and pepper to taste.

**2** Pour the egg on to a large plate and mix the breadcrumbs and half of the Parmesan on another plate. Dip the escalopes first into the egg, then into the breadcrumb mixture to coat well.

**3** Heat the oil in a large frying pan, add the escalopes and fry for 3-4 minutes on each side until golden brown.

**4** Arrange the escalopes in a shallow ovenproof dish, interleaving them with the Mozzarella and tomato slices. Scatter the remaining Parmesan on top and cook in the oven at 200°C/400°F/ Gas Mark 6 for 10-15 minutes until the cheese has melted and the top is beginning to brown. Serve at once.

TOP Parmesan Veal
BOTTOM Saltimbocca

# ITALIAN-STYLE BRAISED PORK

### SERVES 8

| |
|---|
| 1½ × 15 ml tbs vegetable oil |
| 40 g (1½ oz) butter |
| 2.7 kg (6 lb) loin of pork, boned, rinded and tied into a neat joint |
| 3 garlic cloves, skinned and crushed |
| 2 small onions, skinned and chopped |
| 900 ml (1½ pt) milk |
| 7 juniper berries |
| 3 rosemary sprigs |
| salt and pepper |
| 150 ml (5 fl oz) double cream |
| fresh bay leaves, to garnish |

**1** Heat the oil and the butter in a large saucepan or flameproof casserole into which the meat will just fit. Fry the pork, garlic and onion for about 15 minutes or until the pork is browned on all sides. Add the milk, juniper berries, rosemary and seasoning.

**2** Bring to the boil, cover, turn the heat down and cook for about 1½ hours or until the pork is tender, turning and basting from time to time.

**3** Transfer the pork to a warmed serving dish, remove the string and carve into thick slices. Keep warm. The milky cooking juices will look curdled, so rub the sauce through a sieve. Return the sauce to the saucepan, skim off any fat, then stir in the cream. Bring to the boil and simmer for about 5 minutes until slightly reduced. Taste and adjust the seasoning. Pour a little of the sauce over the pork and serve the remaining sauce separately. Garnish with bay leaves.

Italian-style Braised Pork

# LEMON-ROASTED PORK WITH GARLIC AND BASIL

### SERVES 6

| |
|---|
| 2 pork tenderloins, about 335 g (12 oz) each |
| 4 lemons |
| 6 × 15 ml tbs chopped fresh basil or parsley |
| 12 garlic cloves, skinned |
| salt and pepper |
| 2-3 fresh bay leaves |
| 2 × 15 ml tbs oil |
| sautéed shallots, to serve |
| fresh bay leaves, to garnish |

**1** Trim the pork of excess fat. Make a deep cut lengthways into each fillet and open out flat. Grate the rind of four lemons over the pork, then sprinkle with the basil. Cut any large garlic

cloves in half and lay them evenly down the middle of each fillet. Season with salt and pepper to taste.

**2** Close the tenderloins and tie loosely at 2.5 cm (1 in) intervals with string. Place in a shallow, non-metallic dish with the bay leaves and the strained juice of all the lemons. Cover and marinate in the refrigerator overnight.

**3** Remove the pork and reserve the marinade. Heat the oil in a frying pan, add the meat and fry until evenly browned. Transfer to a shallow

Lemon-roasted Pork with Garlic and Basil

roasting tin with the marinade. Season and cook at 200°C/400°F/Gas Mark 6 for 35 minutes, basting frequently, or place on a barbecue and grill for 30-35 minutes, turning frequently, and brushing with the marinade until the pork is cooked through.

**4** To serve, remove the string, then slice the pork and arrange on a bed of sautéed shallots. Garnish with bay leaves.

# FRESH SEAFOOD STEW

SERVES 6

4 × 15 ml tbs olive oil

900 g (2 lb) onions, skinned and finely sliced

450 g (1 lb) thick cod fillets, skinned and cut into 5 cm (2 in) pieces

225 g (8 oz) plaice fillets, skinned and quartered

175 g (6 oz) peeled tiger prawns

salt and pepper

450 g (1 lb) plum tomatoes, skinned, seeded and chopped

2 × 15 ml tbs tomato purée

4 × 15 ml tbs chopped fresh parsley

2 × 15 ml tbs chopped fresh marjoram or oregano

150 ml (5 fl oz) dry white wine

227 g pack ready-prepared seafood cocktail

oregano leaves, to garnish

1 Heat half the oil in a large ovenproof casserole and cook the onions over a low heat for 5 minutes until softened. Using a slotted spoon, lift out about half of the onions and set aside. Spread the remainder evenly over the base of the casserole, then cover with half the fish and prawns – do not add any of the seafood cocktail yet. Season well with salt and pepper to taste.

2 Cover with half of the tomatoes and tomato purée, then repeat the layers. Sprinkle the herbs on top and pour the wine over. Drizzle the remaining oil on top and cook, uncovered, over a very low heat for about 30 minutes or until the liquid has thickened slightly. Stir in the seafood cocktail and heat through for 3-5 minutes. Garnish with oregano leaves.

# TROUT WITH POTATOES GENOESE-STYLE

SERVES 4

450 g (1 lb) unpeeled potatoes, finely sliced

4 × 15 ml tbs olive oil

3 garlic cloves, skinned and crushed

6 × 15 ml tbs chopped fresh parsley

salt and pepper

4 large trout fillets

1 Wash the potatoes in cold water, then pat dry with absorbent kitchen paper. Place the potatoes in a shallow ovenproof dish large enough to take the trout fillets in one layer. Whisk together the olive oil, garlic and parsley and spoon half of this dressing over the potatoes. Season generously with salt and pepper and mix thoroughly.

2 Spread out the potatoes in an even layer in the dish and bake in the oven at 220°C/425°F/Gas Mark 7 for 25 minutes. Remove the dish from the oven and arrange the trout fillets on top of the potatoes.

3 Spoon the remaining olive oil mixture over the trout and potatoes and adjust the seasoning. Return to the oven for 10-12 minutes, basting the fish and potatoes once or twice with the juices, until the trout is cooked through.

TOP Trout with Potatoes Genoese-style
BOTTOM Fresh Seafood Stew

# Vegetable Dishes

*What could be easier than cooking Italian-style when it comes to vegetable dishes? Just think of the dazzling array of colours and shapes, and the wonderful flavours and textures on offer – sun-kissed peppers and tomatoes, glossy-skinned aubergines and courgettes, plump Florence fennel and globe artichokes, tender asparagus … Small wonder the Italians have created such mouthwatering classics for us to enjoy.*

# AUBERGINES WITH MOZZARELLA

SERVES 4–6

*900 g (2 lb) long medium aubergines*

*salt and pepper*

*olive oil*

*1 quantity Tomato Sauce (see page 19)*

*225 g (8 oz) Italian Mozzarella cheese, drained and cubed*

*a handful of fresh basil leaves, marjoram or oregano (optional)*

*1 × 15 ml tbs freshly grated Parmesan cheese*

1  Trim off the ends of the aubergines and discard. Cut the aubergines lengthways into thin slices. Sprinkle the slices generously with salt and leave to drain in a colander for at least 30 minutes.

2  Rinse the aubergines and pat dry with absorbent kitchen paper. Heat a little olive oil in a non-stick frying pan and fry the aubergines, in batches, for 3-4 minutes each side, or until golden brown and just cooked through, brushing the frying pan with more olive oil between each batch. Drain well on crumpled absorbent kitchen paper.

3  Spread half the Tomato Sauce in the base of a large gratin dish. Cover with half the aubergine slices and scatter the Mozzarella on top. Cover with the remaining aubergine slices and sprinkle with herbs, if using. Season with salt and pepper to taste.

4  Spread the remaining Tomato Sauce over the aubergines and sprinkle with Parmesan cheese. Bake in the oven at 200°C/400°F/Gas Mark 6 for 30-35 minutes or until golden brown and bubbling. Leave to cool for 5 minutes before serving.

# PEPERONATA

SERVES 4

*2 small red peppers, quartered and seeded*

*2 small yellow peppers, quartered and seeded*

*2 small green peppers, quartered and seeded*

*4 × 15 ml tbs olive oil*

*2 large onions, skinned and finely sliced*

*1 garlic clove, skinned and crushed*

*450 g (1 lb) plum tomatoes, skinned, seeded and quartered lengthways*

*2 × 15 ml tbs balsamic vinegar*

*10 black olives, stoned and halved*

*salt and pepper*

1  Cut the pepper quarters in half lengthways and set aside. Heat the oil in a large heavy-based frying pan, add the onions and cook for 5 minutes until softened. Add the garlic and peppers to the pan and cook for 10-12 minutes, stirring occasionally, until the peppers are beginning to soften.

2  Stir in the tomatoes and cook gently for 10 minutes. Add the vinegar and olives and season with salt and pepper. Serve the peppers hot or cold, either on their own or as an accompaniment to a main course.

COOK'S TIP

Balsamic vinegar, from Modena, Italy is mellow with a sweet and sour flavour and syrupy consistency. Use it to add piquancy to salad dressings and sauces. Or sprinkle a few drops over meat and fish dishes just before serving. Balsamic vinegar is quite strong so use it sparingly.

Aubergines with Mozzarella

# BAKED STUFFED ARTICHOKES

SERVES 4

| |
|---|
| 4 globe artichokes |
| a little lemon juice |
| 1 egg, beaten |
| 50 g (2 oz) fresh breadcrumbs |
| 115 g (4 oz) Parmesan cheese, grated |
| 2 × 15 ml tbs capers, rinsed |
| 3 canned anchovy fillets, drained and finely chopped |
| 2 garlic cloves, skinned and crushed |
| 3 × 15 ml tbs mixed chopped fresh parsley and mint |
| salt and pepper |
| 3 × 15 ml tbs olive oil |
| 300 ml (10 fl oz) water |

1 Remove and discard all the hard exterior leaves of the artichokes, then cut off the stalks. Slice about 2.5 cm (1 in) from the top of each artichoke, then cut off all the sharp points from the leaves.

2 Open out the artichokes and remove the very small pale leaves from the centre, then scrape away the hairy 'choke' beneath them. Drop the artichokes into a bowl of water and add the lemon juice. Set aside while making the stuffing.

3 Mix together the egg, breadcrumbs, cheese, capers, anchovies, garlic and herbs. Add salt and pepper to taste. Drain the artichokes. Divide the filling amongst them, then arrange upright in a heavy-based saucepan.

4 Drizzle the oil over the top and pour the water into the pan. Bring to the boil, then cover the pan, reduce the heat and simmer gently for about 40 minutes until the artichokes are tender and the water has almost all evaporated. (If the artichokes take longer to cook you may have to add a little extra water). Serve at once.

# STUFFED HERB TOMATOES

SERVES 4

| |
|---|
| 4 large ripe beefsteak tomatoes |
| salt and pepper |
| 3 × 15 ml tbs chopped fresh parsley |
| 2 × 15 ml tbs chopped fresh basil |
| 1 × 15 ml tbs chopped fresh mint |
| 4 × 15 ml tbs coarsely grated Parmesan cheese |
| 6 × 15 ml tbs fresh breadcrumbs |
| 2 × 15 ml tbs olive oil |

1 Cut the tomatoes in half horizontally, then carefully scoop out the insides of the tomatoes with a sharp-edged teaspoon. Sprinkle the insides of the tomatoes with a little salt and stand upside down on absorbent kitchen paper. Leave to drain.

2 Mix together the herbs, Parmesan and breadcrumbs and season with salt and pepper to taste. Arrange the tomato halves in an oiled ovenproof dish and fill with the breadcrumb stuffing.

3 Drizzle the oil over the top and bake in the oven at 200°C/400°F/Gas Mark 6 for 20-25 minutes until the tomatoes are tender and the topping is golden brown. Serve hot or just warm.

Stuffed Herb Tomatoes

# LEMON BAKED FENNEL

### SERVES 4

*675 g (1½ lb) Florence fennel*

*salt and pepper*

*75 g (3 oz) butter*

*finely grated zest of 1 large thin-skinned lemon*

*2 × 15 ml tbs fresh lemon juice*

**1** Trim the base and top stems of the fennel, reserving some of the feathery green tops. Quarter each head lengthways. Blanch in boiling salted water for 5 minutes.

**2** Melt the butter in a shallow flameproof casserole. Remove from the heat, and then add the lemon zest together with the lemon juice. Season with salt and pepper to taste.

**3** Arrange the fennel in the casserole in a single layer, coating in the butter. Cover tightly with a lid or kitchen foil and bake in the oven at 150°C/300°F/Gas Mark 2 for about 1¼ hours. Garnish with snipped fennel tops. Serve hot

# ITALIAN-STYLE PEAS WITH LEEKS

### SERVES 6

*3 × 15 ml tbs olive oil*

*115 g (4 oz) leeks, thinly sliced*

*25 g (1 oz) smoked streaky bacon (about 2-3 thin slices), finely chopped*

*450 g (1 lb) petits pois*

*115 ml (4 fl oz) chicken stock*

*salt and pepper*

**1** Heat the olive oil in a large frying pan and add the leeks and bacon. Cook, stirring, over moderate heat for 1-2 minutes.

**2** Add the peas and stock and season with salt and pepper. Cover and simmer gently for 3-4 minutes until the peas are cooked.

### COOK'S TIP

For a more peppery flavour, try using thinly-sliced pepperoni sausage instead of the bacon. Pepperoni is a pork and beef sausage with red pepper added. Its hot, distinctive taste makes it an excellent ingredient for spicing up risottos and pizza toppings.

Lemon Baked Fennel

TOP Italian-style Peas with Leeks BOTTOM Courgettes Tortino

# COURGETTES TORTINO

SERVES 4

*6 large courgettes, cut diagonally into 0.6 cm (¼ in)
thick slices*

*3 × 15 ml tbs seasoned flour*

*3 × 15 ml tbs olive oil*

*4 eggs, beaten*

*6 × 15 ml tbs milk*

*1 × 15 ml tbs chopped fresh marjoram or oregano*

*3 × 15 ml tbs chopped fresh parsley*

*75 g (3 oz) Parmesan cheese, grated*

*salt and pepper*

*2 × 15 ml tbs fresh breadcrumbs*

**1** Coat the courgette slices in the flour. Heat the oil in a large frying pan, add the courgettes and fry for 8-10 minutes until golden.

**2** Meanwhile, beat together the eggs, milk, herbs and one third of the Parmesan, then season with salt and pepper to taste.

**3** Arrange half of the courgettes in a shallow ovenproof dish. Scatter over another third of Parmesan, then pour half of the egg mixture over. Arrange the remaining courgettes on top and pour the rest of the egg mixture over.

**4** Mix together the breadcrumbs and the remaining Parmesan and scatter over the top. Bake in the oven at 190°C/375°F/Gas Mark 5 for 30-35 minutes until the egg has set.

# POTATO SALAD WITH CAPERS

SERVES 4

| |
|---|
| 675 g (1½ lb) waxy potatoes, scrubbed not peeled |
| 6 × 15 ml tbs olive oil |
| 2 × 15 ml tbs lemon juice |
| 1 small onion, skinned and finely chopped |
| 1 garlic clove, skinned and crushed |
| 1 × 15 ml tbs capers, chopped |
| salt and pepper |
| anchovy fillets and capers, to garnish |

**1** Cook the potatoes gently in their skins in boiling salted water for about 15 minutes, or until just tender. Drain the potatoes and leave until just cool enough to handle. Peel off the skins with your fingers.
**2** Make the dressing. In a large bowl, whisk together the oil and lemon juice until thick. Stir in the onion, garlic and capers.
**3** Pour the dressing over the potatoes whilst they are still warm. Toss well and leave for about 30 minutes until completely cold. Taste and adjust seasoning before serving. Garnish with anchovy fillets and capers.

# MARINATED MUSHROOM SALAD

SERVES 4

| |
|---|
| 6 × 15 ml tbs olive oil |
| 2 × 15 ml tbs lemon juice |
| salt and pepper |
| 225 g (8 oz) button mushrooms, wiped |
| 8 anchovy fillets, soaked in milk (optional) |
| 2 × 15 ml tbs chopped fresh parsley, to garnish |
| herb bread, to serve |

**1** Make the dressing. In a medium bowl, mix together the olive oil, lemon juice and freshly ground pepper. (Do not add salt at this stage if you are using anchovies.)
**2** Slice the mushrooms finely, then add to the dressing and mix well to coat evenly. Cover and leave to stand in a cool place for at least 2 hours.
**3** Just before serving, chop the anchovy fillets, if using, and stir into the mushrooms. Check the seasoning, garnish with the chopped parsley and serve with herb bread.

# SWEET-PEPPER RELISH

SERVES 4–6

| |
|---|
| 3 × 15 ml tbs olive oil |
| 3 large red or yellow peppers, about 450 g (1 lb) total weight, halved, seeded and finely chopped |
| 75 g (3 oz) shallots or onion, skinned and finely chopped |
| 200 ml (7 fl oz) vegetable stock |
| salt and pepper |
| 200 ml (7 fl oz) dry white wine |
| 2 × 15 ml tbs caster sugar |

**1** Heat the olive oil in a medium saucepan, add the peppers and shallots and cook gently, stirring occasionally, until the vegetables are just beginning to soften.
**2** Add all the remaining ingredients and simmer for 15-20 minutes until the mixture is soft. Season with salt and pepper to taste and serve hot or cold.

TOP Potato Salad with Capers
BOTTOM Marinated Mushroom Salad

# DESSERTS

*And finally … here is a collection of tempting desserts to give the final flourish to just about any meal. The recipes include some traditional favourites like the Florentine tipsy cake, Zuccotta, just perfect for special occasions, or Crema Fritta for less formal times. You will also find a rich and heavenly ice cream flavoured with amaretti and toasted almonds; a deliciously-stylish orange and chocolate pasta dish; and some wonderful fruit desserts rich with liqueur.*

OPPOSITE
TOP Zuccotta
BOTTOM Baked Peaches with Ricotta and Almonds

# ROSEMARY FIGS

SERVES 6

| |
|---|
| 2 × 15 ml tbs caster sugar |
| 750 ml (1¼ pt) water |
| grated rind and juice of ½ a lemon |
| 1 sprig of rosemary |
| 450 g (1 lb) dried figs |
| 2 × 15 ml tbs rum |
| double cream, to serve |
| lemon rind, to decorate |

**1** Place the sugar in a pan with the water. Heat until the sugar has dissolved, then add the lemon rind, juice, rosemary and figs.
**2** Simmer gently for about 20 minutes until the figs are plump. Carefully remove the figs to a serving dish. Boil the liquid rapidly until reduced and slightly syrupy. Strain, stir in the rum, and pour over figs. Leave to cool. Serve with cream and decorate with lemon rind.

# BAKED PEACHES WITH RICOTTA AND ALMONDS

SERVES 4

| |
|---|
| 115 g (4 oz) ricotta cheese |
| 50 g (2 oz) ground almonds |
| 2 × 15 ml tbs almond-flavoured liqueur |
| 2 egg whites |
| 115 g (4 oz) caster sugar |
| 4 large peaches, halved and stoned |
| 25 g (1 oz) flaked almonds |

**1** Mix together the ricotta cheese, ground almonds and liqueur. In a separate bowl, whisk the egg whites until they form soft peaks, then whisk in the sugar until stiff. Fold the egg white mixture into the ricotta and almonds and pile into the peach halves.
**2** Scatter the flaked almonds over the top of the stuffed peaches, then arrange in an ovenproof dish. Bake at 200°C/400°F/Gas Mark 6 for 15-20 minutes until the peaches are tender and the topping golden brown. Serve hot.

# ITALIAN PLUMS IN BRANDY

MAKES ABOUT 450 g (1 lb)

| |
|---|
| about 450 g (1 lb) ripe plums |
| 4 whole cloves |
| 1 cinnamon stick |
| 200 g (7 oz) sugar |
| about 300 ml (10 fl oz) brandy |

**1** Wash and dry the plums. Put them in a sterilised airtight Kilner or screwtop 1 lt (1¾ pt) glass jar, packing them right to the top. Add the cloves, cinnamon stick and sugar.
**2** Pour in enough brandy to come to the top of the jar and completely cover the fruit. Seal. Leave for at least 3 months before using, shaking the jar gently from time to time during the first month.

COOK'S TIP

In Italy a strong spirit known as grappa is traditionally used for this recipe, but a low-priced brandy makes a perfectly suitable substitute.

LEFT Rosemary Figs
RIGHT Italian Plums in Brandy

# ORANGE RAVIOLI WITH CHOCOLATE

## SERVES 4

| |
|---|
| 200 g (7 oz) plain flour |
| 2 × size 3 eggs |
| 3 large oranges |
| 115 g (4 oz) plain chocolate, coarsely grated |
| 50 g (2 oz) mascarpone cheese |
| 115 g (4 oz) sugar |
| 1.8 lt (3 pt) water |
| 50 g (2 oz) butter |
| 2 × 15 ml tbs caster sugar |
| 2 × 15 ml tbs orange-flavoured liqueur |
| 2 × 15 ml tbs double cream |
| orange wedges, to decorate |

**1** Heap all but 2 × 15 ml tbs of the flour on to a work surface and make a well in the centre. Break the eggs into the well, then add the grated rind of 2 of the oranges. Work in the flour with your fingers to form a dough, adding a little more flour if it is too sticky. Knead the dough for 5-8 minutes until it becomes smooth and elastic.

**2** Leave the dough to rest, covered with a tea-towel, for 15 minutes, then roll out thinly to a rectangle on a lightly floured board. Fold the dough in half and give it a half turn. Continue rolling and folding in this way until the dough begins to 'pop', then roll out thinly to a large rectangle, about 30 × 60 cm (12 × 24 in) and cut in half.

**3** Reserve 3 × 15 ml tbs of the chocolate, then mix the rest with the mascarpone cheese and spoon about 30 mounds, evenly spaced, on to one sheet of pasta. Brush water around the mounds of filling, then lay the second sheet on top. Press down the pasta around the mounds of filling to seal, then cut into squares using a sharp knife or a fluted pastry wheel.

**4** Place the sugar in a large saucepan with the water and heat gently until the sugar dissolves.

Bring to the boil and add the pasta. Cook for 5-8 minutes until *al dente* (tender but slightly firm), then tip out into a colander to drain thoroughly.

**5** Cut fine shreds of rind from the third orange using a zester and set aside. Squeeze the juice from all the oranges and pour into a saucepan. Add the butter and caster sugar and bring to the boil. Add the ravioli and simmer gently for 10 minutes. Add the liqueur, allow to cool and leave to marinate for at least 1 hour.

**6** To serve, reheat gently, then stir in the double cream. Spoon the ravioli into a serving dish, scatter the reserved chocolate and the orange rind shreds over the top and serve at once, decorated with orange wedges.

# FRUIT SALAD WITH MARASCHINO

## SERVES 6

| |
|---|
| 300 ml (10 fl oz) freshly squeezed orange juice |
| grated rind and juice of 1 lemon |
| 225 g (8 oz) green seedless grapes, washed |
| 4 apricots, halved, stoned and sliced |
| 2 bananas, peeled and thickly sliced |
| 3 red plums, halved, stoned and sliced |
| 40 g (1½ oz) caster sugar |
| 6 × 15 ml tbs maraschino liqueur |

**1** Pour the orange juice into a large bowl, add the lemon rind and juice, then stir in all of the fruit. Add the sugar and maraschino and mix thoroughly.

**2** Cover and chill in the refrigerator for at least 4 hours, or overnight. Remove and stir well before serving.

TOP Fruit Salad with Maraschino
BOTTOM Orange Ravioli with Chocolate

# CREMA FRITTA

SERVES 4–6

| |
|---|
| *3 eggs* |
| *50 g (2 oz) caster sugar* |
| *50 g (2 oz) plain flour, sifted* |
| *225 ml (8 fl oz) milk* |
| *300 ml (10 fl oz) single cream* |
| *finely grated rind of ½ a lemon* |
| *115 g (4 oz) dry white breadcrumbs* |
| *vegetable oil, for shallow frying* |
| *caster sugar, to serve* |

**1** In a large bowl, beat 2 eggs and the sugar together until the mixture is pale. Add the flour, beating all the time, and then, very slowly, beat in the milk and cream. Add the lemon rind.

**2** Pour the mixture into a buttered shallow 18 cm (7 in) square cake tin. Bake in the oven at 180°C/350°F/Gas Mark 4 for about 1 hour, until a skewer inserted in the middle comes out clean. Leave to cool for 2-3 hours, or preferably overnight.

**3** When completely cold, cut into sixteen cubes and remove from the cake tin. Beat the remaining egg in a bowl. Dip the cubes in the egg and then in the breadcrumbs until well coated.

**4** Heat the oil in a frying pan and when hot, slide in the cubes. Fry for 2-3 minutes until golden brown and a crust is formed. Turn and fry the second side. Drain well on absorbent kitchen paper. Serve immediately, sprinkled with caster sugar.

Crema Fritta

# GENOESE APPLE TORTA

SERVES 6

| |
|---|
| *4 eggs* |
| *150 g (5 oz) caster sugar* |
| *150 g (5 oz) plain flour* |
| *1 × 5 ml tsp baking powder* |
| *pinch of salt* |
| *115 g (4 oz) butter, melted and cooled* |
| *6 × 15 ml tbs milk* |
| *finely grated rind of 1 lemon* |
| *675 g (1½ lb) dessert apples, such as Golden Delicious, peeled, cored and thinly sliced* |
| *1-2 × 15 ml tbs vegetable oil* |
| *1-2 × 15 ml tbs dried breadcrumbs* |
| *icing sugar, to finish (optional)* |

**1** Put the eggs and sugar in a heatproof bowl standing over a pan of gently simmering water. Whisk for 10-15 minutes until the mixture is thick and pale and holds a ribbon trail when the beaters are lifted. (Alternatively, if you have a table-top electric mixer, this can be used instead of whisking over hot water.)

**2** Remove the bowl from the heat and continue

Genoese Apple Torta

whisking until the mixture is cool. Sift the flour with the baking powder and salt. Using a large metal spoon, fold half of this mixture gently into the whisked eggs and sugar.

**3** Slowly trickle the melted butter around the edge of the bowl and fold it in gently. Take care not to stir too heavily or the mixture will lose air. Fold in the remaining flour mixture, then the milk and lemon rind and finally the apples.

**4** Brush the inside of a 23 cm (9 in) diameter cake tin with oil. Sprinkle with breadcrumbs, then shake off the excess. Pour the cake mixture into the tin and bake in the oven at 180°C/350°F/Gas Mark 4 for about 40 minutes until a skewer inserted in the centre comes out clean.

**5** Leave the cake to rest in the tin for about 5 minutes, then turn out on to a wire rack and leave for 2-3 hours to cool completely. Sift icing sugar over the top of the cake just before serving, if wished.

# ZUCCOTTA

SERVES 6–8

| |
|---|
| 50 g (2 oz) blanched almonds |
| 50 g (2 oz) hazelnuts |
| 3 × 15 ml tbs brandy |
| 2 × 15 ml tbs orange-flavoured liqueur |
| 2 × 15 ml tbs cherry- or almond- flavoured liqueur |
| 335 g (12 oz) sponge fingers or trifle sponges, split in half through middle |
| 150 g (5 oz) plain chocolate |
| 425 ml (15 fl oz) double cream |
| 150 g (5 oz) icing sugar |
| chocolate pieces and grated chocolate, to decorate |

1 Spread the almonds and hazelnuts out separately on a baking tray and toast in the oven at 200°C/400°F/Gas Mark 6 for 5 minutes until golden.

2 Transfer the hazelnuts to a clean tea-towel and rub off the skins while still warm. Spread all the nuts out to cool, then roughly chop.

3 Line a 1.2 lt (2 pt) pudding basin or round-bottomed bowl with damp muslin.

4 In a separate bowl, mix together the brandy and the liqueurs. Sprinkle the sponge fingers or split trifle sponges with the brandy and liqueur mixture.

5 Line the basin with the moistened sponges, reserving enough to cover the top.

6 Using a sharp knife, chop 75 g (3 oz) of the plain chocolate into small pieces and set aside.

7 In a separate bowl, whip the cream with 115 g (4 oz) icing sugar until stiff and fold in the chopped chocolate and nuts. Divide this mixture in two and use one half to spread over the sponge lining in an even layer.

8 Melt the remaining chocolate, cool slightly, then fold into the remaining cream mixture. Use this to fill the centre of the pudding.

9 Level the top of the zuccotto and cover with the remaining moistened sponge. Trim edges. Cover and refrigerate for at least 12 hours.

10 Turn the pudding upside down on to a plate and remove the muslin. Dust with the remaining icing sugar and decorate with chocolate pieces and grated chocolate.

# CHOCOLATE 'SALAMI'

SERVES 6–8

| |
|---|
| 50 g (2 oz) split blanched almonds |
| 20 Petit Beurre biscuits |
| 225 g (8 oz) plain chocolate, broken into pieces |
| 175 g (6 oz) unsalted butter, cut into small pieces |
| 3 × 15 ml tbs almond-flavoured liqueur or brandy |
| 25 g (1 oz) ground almonds |

1 Toast the blanched almonds under a moderate grill for a few minutes until evenly browned. Transfer the nuts to a blender or food processor and work until finely ground.

2 Put the biscuits in a heavy bowl and crush roughly with the end of a rolling pin. Take out a handful of the crushed biscuits and set aside.

3 Put the chocolate pieces, butter and liqueur in a large heatproof bowl standing over a pan of gently simmering water. Heat gently until melted, stirring occasionally to combine.

4 Add the melted chocolate mixture to the crushed biscuits and toasted nuts and mix well. Leave in a cool place to firm up.

5 Turn the mixture out on to a large sheet of lightly buttered foil. Shape into a sausage about 23 cm (9 in) long, with tapering ends. Wrap in the foil and freeze for about 4 hours or until solid.

6 Crush the reserved biscuits to a fine powder in an electric blender or food processor, then mix with the ground almonds. Unwrap the 'salami' and roll in the powder until evenly coated. Leave for 1 hour before serving.

Chocolate 'Salami'

# CENCI

MAKES 50

| |
|---|
| 300 g (11 oz) plain flour |
| 2 eggs, beaten |
| 3 × 15 ml tbs rum |
| 4 × 15 ml tbs caster sugar |
| 1 × 5 ml tsp baking powder |
| pinch of salt |
| vegetable oil, for deep frying |
| icing sugar, for sprinkling |

**1** Make the dough. Sift 250 g (9 oz) of the flour into a bowl. Make a well in the centre and add the next five ingredients, mixing them well together with a fork until they come together as a dough.
**2** Sprinkle the work surface with some of the remaining flour. Turn the dough out on to the floured surface and gather into a ball with your fingers. Knead until smooth.
**3** Cut the dough into quarters. Roll out one quarter of the dough until almost paper thin, adding more flour to the work surface as necessary. Cut into strips about 15 cm (6 in) long and 2.5 cm (1 in) wide. Tie the strips into loose knots. Repeat rolling, cutting and tying with the remaining three quarters of dough.
**4** Half-fill a deep-fat fryer with oil and heat to 190°C/375°F or until a cube of day-old bread browns in 40 seconds. Add 4-5 of the pastry twists to the oil and fry for 1-2 minutes until golden. Drain on absorbent kitchen paper while frying the remainder. Sift icing sugar over the twists while they are hot. Serve warm or cold.

# AMARETTI ICE CREAM

SERVES 4

| |
|---|
| 600 ml (20 fl oz) milk |
| 2 × 15 ml tbs custard powder |
| 3 × 15 ml tbs caster sugar |
| 50 g (2 oz) blanched almonds, chopped |
| 150 ml (5 fl oz) double cream |
| 12 Amaretti biscuits, crushed |
| 2 × 15 ml tbs almond-flavoured liqueur |
| Amaretti biscuits, to serve |

**1** Blend a little of the milk with the custard powder and sugar to make a paste, then blend in the rest of the milk. Transfer to a saucepan and bring to the boil, stirring all the time, until boiling and thickened.
**2** Remove the pan from the heat, cover the surface of the custard with a sheet of cling film and leave until cold. Meanwhile, toast the almonds under the grill for 3-5 minutes until golden. Leave to cool.
**3** Whip the cream until it forms soft peaks and fold into the custard with the almonds, crushed Amaretti biscuits and almond-flavoured liqueur. Pour into a freezerproof container and freeze for 2 hours until firm around the edges.
**4** Remove from the freezer and beat well, then return to the freezer and freeze until solid. Twenty minutes before serving, transfer the ice cream to the refrigerator to allow to soften slightly, then scoop into glasses and drizzle a little extra liqueur over each portion. Serve with Amaretti biscuits.

### COOK'S TIP

Amaretti are small, crisp Italian macaroons flavoured with bitter almonds. They are delicious served with after-dinner coffee or used as an ingredient in sweet dishes.

TOP Amaretti Ice Cream
BOTTOM Cenci

# INDEX